REFLECTIONS IN VERSE

Reflections in Verse

REFLECTIONS IN VERSE:
Volume 7
"Vanished Innocence"

KHALILAH H. PURNELL

NYLA Publishing, LLC

Books by Khalilah H. Purnell may be purchased for educational, business, or sales promotional use. For information, please e-mail the publisher/representative for the author at info@khalilahhpurnell.com

Designed by Inked Solace, LLC

Copyedited and published by Nyla Publishing, LLC

Purnell, Khalilah H., author

Series Title: Reflections in Verse / by Khalilah H. Purnell, Volume Title: Vanished Innocence

Description: Newport News, VA: NYLA Publishing, LLC [2023]

Identifiers: ISBN, 9798868990526

Category: Poetry, Adult/General, Inspirational

Dedication

Dedicated to the Missing Black Children,

"In the shadows of our society, you are not forgotten. Your innocence has been stolen, and your voices silenced. This volume is dedicated to you, to bring awareness, understanding, and action. We stand for justice and equality, and the day when your stories are told, your names are known, and your innocence is honored. We are your voice, your advocates, and your protectors. Your existence matters, and we're determined to bring you home. Until that day, we will continue to seek answers, as we search, speak, and fight."

You are the heartbeat of change.

Khalilah H. Purnell

Reflections in Verse

Introduction

In the hushed shadows of innocence, there exists a world where the echoes of missing voices reverberate through the collective conscience. Here, where the brightest stars are the children who have vanished, their stories have been silenced, overshadowed by the noise of daily life. Yet within these pages, we embark on a journey to reignite the forgotten tales, a journey that explores the void left by our missing black children.

Reflections in Verse, Volume 7: Vanishing Innocence opens a portal to a realm where young souls have disappeared without a trace. It delves into the depths of heartache, amplifying their unheard whispers, and seeking to restore the importance of every child's story. As we explore this intricate tapestry of verses, we aim to resuscitate the collective outrage and empathy that the plight of these missing black children deserves.

This collection is more than just a series of poems; it is an anthem for change, a call for recognition, and a tribute to every child whose voice has been muted. It aims to shed light on the prevailing issue of missing black children, offering a manual of understanding that seeks to bridge the divide in levels of priority and respect in these heart-wrenching cases. Through the power of verse, we aspire to create awareness, ignite action, and instigate the transformation our society so desperately needs.

Join us on this poignant journey, as we give voice to the silence, empathy to the suffering, and strength to the disheartened. Vanishing Innocence is an endeavor to ensure that our world never forgets the stories of our missing black children.

Message From the Author:

Dear Readers,

As the ink flows through the pages of Reflections in Verse, Volume 7: Vanishing Innocence, I invite you to partake in a poignant journey to restore the voices of our missing black children. The words in this volume are more than a collection of poems; they are a call to action, an echo for justice, and a testament to the resilience of the human spirit.

In these verses, you'll discover the unwavering strength and unyielding hope that lives within each of us. It is a journey through heartache and healing, an exploration of societal disparities and the power of unity. As you read, let us rekindle the collective conscience and recommit to ensuring that every missing child's story is acknowledged and valued, irrespective of their race.

Thank you for joining me in this critical quest, not just as readers but as advocates for change. Together, we can raise awareness, create empathy, and inspire action. This is a battle we fight with words, but it's also one we fight with hearts united by compassion.

With profound gratitude,

Reflections in Verse

Khalilah H. Purnell

BOOK NAVIGATION

Section 2: Oblivion's Toll: Disappearing Truths

Fading Footprints

Eclipsed Youth: Fading into the Void

Invisible Tears: Truths Buried Deep

Drowned Voices: Unrecognized Pain

Tracing Lost Innocence

Soulful Absence

Vanishing Youth

Truth in Shadows

Eclipsed Horizons: Voices in Darkness

Buried Secrets: Unheard Voices Speak

Gone But Not Forgotten: Missing Reflections

Section 3: Echoes of Exploitation

Taken From Tomorrow

Innocence for Sale

Invisible Chains: Unveiling the Abyss

Rescued Whispers

Section 4: The Silent Epidemic

The Hidden Trade

Bodies for Profit

Pricing Humanity

Stolen Lives, Stolen Organs

Searching for Answers

Black Market Horrors: The Trail of Vanishing Lives

Section 5: Holding the Mirror to Bias

Hidden Realities: Seeking Fairness

Untold Stories: A Quest for Equity

The Missing Headlines

Unseen Pleas: The Media's Silent Lens

Media's Selective Echo

Invisible Crisis: Disparity in Spotlight

Law Enforcement's Apathy

Dismissed Tears: A Cry for Recognition

Searching Alone: Disregarded Cries

Torn Apart: The Battle for Belief

Vanished Innocence

Reflections in Verse

SECTION I: SHADOWS OF NEGLECT

Reflections in Verse

Promise to Pain: Seeking Jelani Day

In the heart of shadows, a tale unfolds,

A story of anguish that slowly erodes,

Jelani Day's name, a whispered refrain,

Bound in a narrative of loss and pain.

In the spring of life, with dreams unconfined,

A student's journey, a brilliant mind.

His promise, like stars in the velvet night,

Fell prey to the enigma that shrouds his light.

Neglect, a haunting specter in the room,

With answers that linger in an eerie gloom.

A mother's plea for truth, steadfast and clear,

Echoes in the abyss, though no one would hear.

From the heart of Chicago to the nation's gaze,

A family's heartache, caught in a daze.

The media's eye wanders elsewhere in its quest,

While Jelani's verity remains unexpressed.

But, oh, Jelani, through this verse, your voice is found,

A search for justice, the truth unbound.

The call for integrity, a beacon burning bright,

Guiding us through the darkest of the night.

The waters may hold secrets, but we shall wade,

Through deep currents, our resolution is displayed.

Your name, once obscured, lost in elusive streams,

With "Promise to Pain," we'll illuminate the schemes.

For your story is intricate, woven with care,

Threads of bias and illusions ensnare.

A labyrinth of questions, we promise to unthread,

To allow your truth and memory to spread.

With each line composed, and every word we confide,

Your promise becomes our objective, our guide.

In this narrative, we unveil your saga's truth,

And venerate your memory, everlasting and uncouth.

In the depths of our yearning, we seek the illumination,

To unfurl the cloak and exalt your narration.

With truth as our compass and justice as our plea,

"Promise to Pain" shall immortalize thee.

Reflections in Verse

Shadows In the Backyard: The Mystery of Danye Jones

Beneath the crescent moon's soft, mournful light,

In his mother's backyard, where day turned to night.

Danye, a young soul in the prime of his years,

Hanging lifeless, amid unspoken fears.

In the quietude of darkness, he found his fate,

Strung up by a sheet, an ominous weight.

Bruises marred his face, a tale left untold,

In the shadows of the backyard, mysteries unfold.

Pants hung at half-mast, yet securely belted tight,

Hands clenched in fists as if to fight the night.

They say he did this to himself, a cruel fabrication,

But the evidence murmurs, another explanation.

Injustice thrives where secrets are concealed,

In the land of the unheard, where truths are revealed.

Danye's voice was silenced, his dreams denied,

In the shadows of that backyard, he desperately cried.

The media's silence, the law's indifference,

Conspired in neglect, a shocking incoherence.

Families like his left searching for the truth,

Amidst the tangled web of injustice, our lost youth.

Danye's mother, a lioness in the face of despair,

Her heart bears the weight of a pain so unfair.

She demanded answers, with relentless persistence,

But found only resistance, and shattered existence.

In the backyard's shadows, the questions remain,

Seeking answers, we'll dissolve the refrain.

To uncover the story, illuminate the dark,

In the shadows of injustice, we'll kindle a spark.

Let's amplify their voices, let the truth resound,

For Danye and his mother, on hallowed ground.

In the shadows of the backyard, the truth awaits,

To finally unveil the truth, of what happened
behind those gates.

Reflections in Verse

The Unsolved Riddle: Kenneka Jenkins Echo

In the Crowne Plaza's hushed halls, she roamed,

A night that left questions, a tragic unknown.

Kenneka, young and vibrant, a life untold,

Within those cold walls, her story would unfold.

They gathered to celebrate, beneath dimmed lights,

In the depths of the night, where mysteries took flight.

But as the hours ticked by, unease did begin,

To shroud the truth within a web of sin.

Alcohol and laughter, in the dim-lit room,

Yet something concealed, impending gloom.

Amid friends and strangers, her path unclear,

Swaying like a reed, her essence they'd smear.

Was it the spirits that led her astray,

Or a sinister hand, that stole her away?

No marijuana, no drugs of that kind,

Still, her life would unwind, enigma enshrined.

In surveillance's gaze, at 3:20 a.m.,

She staggered alone, a question to stem.

A mother's alarm, at the dawn's early light,

Teresa Martin's pursuit, in the quest for what's right.

The lobby she scoured, from top floor to ground,

The echoes of loss, in silence, resound.

Lacking urgency, the initial response,

A mother's anguish, the cost of nonchalance.

At last, on the screen, they found her path,

In the labyrinth's maze, her fleeting aftermath.

A chilling discovery, with heartache replete,

Kenneka's last steps, in the cold's cruel deceit.

Back against the wall, she lay, in a chilling embrace,

One shoe discarded, in that dark and moist place.

No trauma apparent, save a minor wound,

In the moist of confines, where her fate was marooned.

No illegal substances, her blood would attest,

Yet alcohol's presence, in a seemingly cruel twist.

Topiramate, a stranger to her veins,

In a tragic convergence, they'd share the reins.

Hypothermia's onset, in silent cold bloom,

Lesions in her stomach, the cold's silent tomb.

A puzzle unsolved, with facts intertwined,

In the echoes of night, the mystery is confined.

Kenneka's voice lingers, in memory's throes,

A riddle unsolved, where empathy grows.

Her mother, Theresa, relentless and brave,

Seeking the truth, her daughter to save.

In 2023's light, a settlement decree,

For an undisclosed sum, to set spirits free.

No wealth can replace what's forever gone,

But it aids in healing, as they journey on.

"The Unsolved Riddle" of Kenneka's last plea,

Echoes through time, a solemn decree.

Her story persists, an unanswered call,

In the hearts of those who remember all.

Footprints in the Gym: The Kendrick Johnson Tragedy

In the heart of Valdosta, in a school's quiet hall,

A story of young Kendrick, we solemnly recall.

A student, full of promise, in the bloom of his youth,

But beneath those mat-bound footprints, lay a cruel truth.

On that fateful day in 2013's embrace,

Kendrick's life was taken, leaving little trace.

An enigma, a puzzle, a riddle concealed,

In the shadows of the gym, his fate was sealed.

They tried to paint it as an accident, you see,

But the facts spoke louder, to you and to me.

A shoe moved in mystery, contradicting their lies,

For Kendrick's voice to be heard, we must recognize.

The GBI's report, with a narrow view,

Missed blunt force trauma, a fact that's true.

But in the second autopsy, a different story
unfolds,

With traces of brutality, a tale untold.

The organs went missing, disposed without care,

The truth obstructed, a heavy burden to bear.

Surveillance tapes edited, timelines obscure,

Cover-up suspicions, and motives impure.

A lawsuit was filed, the Johnsons in plight,

Demanding answers, in search of the light.

Their quest for justice, relentless and bold,

For the loss of their son, a story to be told.

The echoes of prejudice, injustice's stain,

Lingered in the silence, causing endless pain.

With every U.S. Attorney's mysterious departure,

Questions mounted, revealing a disturbing culture.

In 2016, the DOJ's decision was clear,

No criminal charges, and the family in fear.

They faced legal battles, amidst claims so vast,

An $850,000 fee, and defamation's harsh cast.

A case reopened, hope on the horizon's brink,

Yet Sheriff Paulk's stance made us pause and think.

No claims of wrongdoing, the case not homicide,

Left us with questions that would not subside.

In March of 2021, a glimmer of hope,

As the case was rekindled, we'd strive to cope.

Yet in January 2022, the door seemed to close,

Leaving Kendrick's story, and the pain it imposed.

"Footprints in the Gym," where questions reside,

A son's lost voice, in the truth we confide.

In the labyrinth of injustice, we persist,

To honor Kendrick's memory, our ceaseless tryst.

Reflections in Verse

Silenced Dawn: The Abduction of Ashanti Billie

In the still of the night, her footsteps took flight,

Ashanti Billie, a beacon, a guiding light.

A 19-year-old soul, full of dreams so bright,

But her story took a turn, into the darkest night.

She worked at Blimpie's, a student on her way,

To culinary heights, where her passion would sway.

At Joint Expeditionary Base, she'd start her day,

But on that September morn, she was led astray.

A silent abduction, from her workplace she'd go,

Innocence stolen, a victim of a cruel blow.

Her car found in Norfolk, with clothing to show,

If something sinister happened, the world soon would know.

Days turned to nights, and with heavy hearts, they prayed,

For Ashanti's safe return, with hope that never swayed.

But behind a church in Charlotte, her life had frayed,

A young soul now silenced, in a cold, shallow grave.

Eric Brown, a veteran, a man with a troubled mind,

Charged with kidnapping, his actions were unkind.

Diagnosed with schizophrenia, a life intertwined,

With the tragic fate of Ashanti, and a search they'd never find.

Amid the darkness, her parents took a stand,

With unwavering strength, they'd make a final demand.

The Ashanti Alert Act, a beacon for the land,

To save others from this nightmare, held in the devil's hand.

A voluntary network, a lifeline to create,

For those over 17, a chance to alter fate.

Beyond Amber Alerts, a new hope to contemplate,

Ashanti's legacy lives on, helping hearts navigate.

Silenced dawn, a voice unheard, her story we now share,

To honor her memory, to show that we care.

In the face of tragedy, her parents did bear,

A testament to their strength, a love beyond compare.

In the echoes of her absence, we'll forever hold the key,

To remember Ashanti Billie and the person she could be.

And in her name, we'll strive for change, united, you and me,

For a world where all are safe and truly free.

Reflections in Verse

Whispers in the Wind: The Enigma of Kierra Cole's Disappearance

In the heart of Chicago's bustling embrace,

A postal worker named Kierra, in a vibrant space.

With a future ahead, her dreams held so tight,

She ventured forth in the day and into the night.

Carrying a secret, a life yet to bloom,

A precious life within her, in her motherly womb.

But one fateful day, the world stood still,

As the whispers of her presence vanished, a void to fill.

In 2018, the year etched in the past,

Kierra Coles, her story, a mystery amassed.

A postal worker, a woman with dreams,

Disappeared without a trace, or so it seems.

Her footsteps in the city, a dance on the street,

Yet the truth of that day remains incomplete.

A mother-to-be, with hopes running deep,

The secrets of her absence, a secret they keep.

Five years have passed, the questions persist,

The yearning for answers, a relentless twist.

In the whispers of the wind, her voice finds flight,

A longing for her loved ones, to ease the night.

From the shadows, she speaks, her story untold,

A future unseen, in the tales that unfold.

To her family and friends, in the darkness of despair,

Kierra's voice emerges, a solace they can share.

Beyond the veil, in the realms unseen,

Guiding her loved ones through the places between.

Though her presence they can't embrace,

Her whispers in the wind offer a consoling grace.

Vanished Innocence

The pages of her life, a narrative incomplete,

In the hearts of those who love her, her memory is replete.

In the city of Chicago, where her story resides,

Kierra's whispers bring comfort, where her presence abides.

Her mystery endures, unanswered questions untold,

But her voice in the wind, a story to be extolled.

A voiceless echo, in the whispers of time,

Kierra Coles, her presence, forever in rhyme.

Reflections in Verse

A Journey in the Unknown: Daniel Robinson's Silent Cry

In the heart of the desert's embrace, a geologist's story takes its place,

Daniel Robinson, aged twenty-four, last seen in a vast expanse to explore.

A sunlit morning, his Jeep on the road, towards the horizon, a story untold,

Leaving the job site, a path unknown, a journey into the vast unknown.

A new coworker, a connection just made, their stories, like the earth, freshly laid,

Buckeye, Arizona, where geology thrives, where the desert landscape truly survives.

From Phoenix, he came, a field geologist's dream, graduating in 2019, so it would seem.

June 23, 2021, etched in time, the day Daniel's path would intertwine.

July 19, the Jeep found on its side, in a desert ravine where secrets hide,

Airbags deployed, a seatbelt intact, questions linger, a sense of impact.

His belongings scattered, his cell, his keys, a scene that beckons, a sense of unease,

The search began, hope and despair, as Daniel's presence filled the desert air.

Late July, a skull found in the sand, hopes rose and fell with the arid land,

Yet, testing revealed it wasn't his face, a moment in time, a somber space.

The Buckeye Police claimed to strive, 70 square miles they tried to drive,

With UTVs, cadaver dogs, and more, the desert's secrets they aimed to explore.

A private investigator, a father's quest, suggesting the scene was not like the rest,

The accident staged the ignition's turn, unanswered questions for which they yearn.

Over 11 miles registered on that day, a riddle unwrapped, a price to pay,

Robinson's father's voice echoed in the heat, a father's love, a relentless beat.

A stark contrast painted in black and white, the national stage's unequal light,

The spotlight dim on stories like these, while others shine with greater ease.

A voice from the desert, echoing true, of Daniel's journey and what he went through,

In the vast unknown, he seeks his way, a journey we remember, come what may.

Reflections in Verse

Shadows of the Unforgotten: The Search for Keeshae Jacobs

In shadows cast by the unforgiving years,

A mother's voice, unheard, a sea of tears,

Six years have passed, and still, she waits in vain,

For answers to end her heart's ceaseless pain.

Keeshae, a name etched in the city's heart,

Vanished one day, torn worlds torn apart,

On Church Hill's streets, she last was seen,

Now lost in time, a nightmare unforeseen.

A man named Tucker, the key to the truth,

But tales he weaves, no justice, no sleuth,

The last to see her, or so he claims,

With secrets buried deep, hiding his games.

A home search request, red flags raised high,

Why summon another detective's eye?

Connections hidden in the shadows deep,

A puzzle unsolved, secrets it keeps.

Her mother fights with a relentless fire,
Her love and strength will never tire,
Seeking the truth, a daughter to find,
A mission of the heart, her soul aligned.

Re-open the case, foundation's hand,
Extends its reach across the land,
Together they strive for justice's grace,
To find Keeshae, to see her face.

In shadows of the unforgotten years,
A plea for answers, a mother's tears,
Six years have passed, but still, they fight,
To bring Keeshae's story back into the light.

A Cry Unanswered: Searching for Lashaya

In the stillness of the night, her fate unknown,

Lashaya, vibrant soul, a story to be shown,

A mother's worry, a community's despair,

Her presence vanished into the night's cold air.

Aurora, her home, a place of dreams,

Where life's potential gleams in youthful beams,

But that fateful night, she slipped away,

Into the dark, where shadows held their sway.

The night's silence whispered secrets untold,

As young Lashaya walked those streets, so bold,

No phone, no wallet, plans to return,

Yet something in the night began to churn.

Surveillance eyes caught her on that street,

The final trace of her, where paths did meet,

A young girl lost in the world's cruel sweep,

While others lay in tranquil, dream-filled sleep.

To authorities, a runaway, they claimed,

Injustice in assumptions, her family blamed,

For Lashaya was more than just statistics cold,

A bright future, a story yet to unfold.

Days passed by, but still, she did not return,

Inquiry and concern, lessons we must learn,

For in cases like these, we must unite,

And amplify each voice, shine a guiding light.

A mother's plea, a community's pain,

To find young Lashaya and break this chain,

Of assumptions that ignore the truth,

Those lives are worth more than our youth.

Through the years, tips trickled in like rain,

A hope of answers, a way to ease the pain,

In that place where shadows seem to dwell,

Her spirit lingers, and the stories tell.

On Colfax Avenue, they sought a trace,

Of Lashaya's presence, in that shadowed space,

A captive soul, in the motel room they found,

But the puzzle's pieces still lay all around.

A cry unanswered, yet hope prevails,

In the unity of voices, the truth unveils,

Lashaya's story, her memory we keep,

In our hearts, forever, her spirit runs deep.

Reflections in Verse

The Paradox of an 'Ebony Alert'

In the realm of urgency, where shadows cast their pall,

A new creation takes its form, to answer the call.

An "Ebony Alert" they say, for lives that disappear,

But do we question its true intent, the purpose that's unclear?

Will it be a beacon bright, to guide those lost in night?

Or deepen the divides we face, exacerbate the fight?

The paradox of "Ebony Alert," it hangs before our eyes,

A double-edged sword, it seems, beneath the darkened skies.

Will this new creation amplify the voices we've oppressed,

Or further drown the cries for help, in apathy's cruel jest?

As we ponder this conundrum, in search of truth we strive,

For unity and justice, we must keep hope alive.

In the paradox of "Ebony Alert," let's hope for equity,

A world where race and color, no longer blind our eyes to see,

That every missing soul, regardless of their face,

Deserves our swift attention, a fair and equal chase.

So, let us question, let us learn, as the "Ebony Alert" takes flight,

For in our collective wisdom, we can make what's wrong seem right.

And as we stand together, in the struggle we'll take part,

To ensure that every life is cherished, from the heart.

SECTION 2: OBLIVION'S TOLL: DISAPPEARING TRUTHS

Reflections in Verse

Fading Footprints

In the realm of shadows, where secrets softly weep,

A trail of fading footprints in the sands of time so deep.

Oblivion's toll on vanished youth, the echoes of despair,

As innocence is swallowed by the void, leaving hearts laid bare.

The footprints disappear like whispers lost in the wind,

As we seek to understand, to unravel what's chagrined.

A story told in silent steps, of those who've slipped away,

Their fading footprints beckon us, to shine a guiding ray.

In the obscurity of life's regrets, where truth begins to fade,

We yearn to grasp the meaning of the choices we have made.

Oblivion's toll, takes its hold, as fading footprints wane,

But in the verses of our hearts, their memory will remain.

Let's not forget the innocence, that vanished with the night,

But cherish every fleeting step, in the realm of fading light.

For in these fading footprints, there's a lesson to be learned,

A chance to find redemption, as the pages of life are turned.

Eclipsed Youth: Fading into the Void

In a world where dreams should soar and fly,

The young, the hopeful, with stars in their eye,

But within this narrative, their voices, a void,

A generation eclipsed; their stories destroyed.

They once were the promise of brighter days,

With endless potential in countless ways.

Yet their paths grew dim, their presence
concealed,

Their innocence lost, their fate long since sealed.

Each day, the sun rises, but their light remains
gone,

In the shadows they dwell, silenced and
withdrawn.

As we gather the fragments of their whispered
tales,

A haunting reality behind each silent wail.

They walked the same streets, under the same sky,

As you and me, they dreamed and wondered why.

But their youth, like eclipses, passed into the dark,

Their voices unheard, leaving an indelible mark.

The void swallows their stories, like secrets untold,

As the world moves forward, their presence grows cold.

Yet in our hearts, we remember their names,

Their smiles, their laughter, their vibrant flames.

For they were more than just statistics or trends,

Their journeys, their hopes, their lives, their friends.

In this story of youth, forever eclipsed,

Their memories persist, though in void they're adrift.

Their faces may fade, their voices may cease,

But the impact they left grant us no release.

As we honor their lives and remember their grace,

In the void, they're a light, a resilient embrace.

So let us speak their names, keep their stories alive,

Amidst the void's silence, their spirits survive.

In a world where their youth was cruelly denied,

We'll remember these lives, forever by their side.

Reflections in Verse

Invisible Tears: Truths Buried Deep

Invisible tears, truths buried deep,

A haunting silence, secrets they keep.

Innocence stolen, voices concealed,

In the shadows of life, their pain revealed.

They walked this earth, like you and me,

Dreams in their hearts, visions to be.

Yet their stories untold, their struggles concealed,

Invisible tears, the scars unhealed.

The world moves on, unaware of their plight,

As they fade from our view, lost in the night.

But their presence remains, in the depths of our souls,

Invisible tears, their stories unfold.

The truth lies buried beneath the ground,

Invisible tears, where no solace is found.

But we'll dig deep, uncover each face,

Remember their lives, in this sacred space.

Invisible tears, let them no longer hide,

The pain and the suffering they felt inside.

For in speaking their names, their stories we share,

Invisible tears, we show that we care.

In the still of the night, their whispers we'll keep,

Invisible tears are no longer buried deep.

Their voices will rise, their truth will be heard,

Invisible tears, we'll honor each word.

Drowned Voices: Unrecognized Pain

In the stillness of the night, a somber truth we
must embrace,

The voices of our youth, now lost without a trace,

They once walked among us, with dreams and
hopes untamed,

But now their voices are silenced, by a world that
seems untamed.

Their laughter once like music, in the playgrounds
they would play,

Now echoes in the memories, of those left to
mourn their day,

For each one has a story, a future yet unwritten,

But in this cruel oblivion, their voices have been
smitten.

They vanish from the streets, from the
neighborhoods we roam,

Invisible to many, as if they're far from home,

Their faces on the posters, their names engraved
in tears,

But will we ever find them, and calm their darkest fears?

The system may forget them, but we won't let them go,

We'll fight to keep their voices alive, to make their stories known,

In unity, we stand, together we will fight,

To bring our children back from the depths of endless night.

For they are not forgotten, their voices still resound,

We'll search for them tirelessly until they all are found,

In the quiet of the night, we'll listen to their cries,

And together we'll ensure their voices never die.

Tracing Lost Innocence

In shadows deep, where innocence hides,

The echoes of youth, in silence, subsides.

A story unfolds, a narrative untold,

Of young souls vanishing, lost in the cold.

Black lives, like stars, often unseen,

Fading away in a world so keen,

To overlook the pain and despair,

Of families searching, burdened to bear.

Drowned voices in the sea of despair,

Their stories untold, life's unfair affair,

Invisible tears and silent cries,

As our youth vanish, their dreams arise.

Why does the world turn a blind eye,

To the ones who suffer, to the question why?

In the void, their names are often erased,

Their presence denied, their memory misplaced.

But we will not forget, we'll search, and we'll find,

The lost innocence of youth left behind,

In unity and strength, we'll raise our voice,

To trace their existence, to make the choice.

To bring back the ones who've disappeared,

To end the indifference, to make it clear,

Black lives matter, and we'll never cease,

To search for our youth and find their peace.

In the echoes of the past and the cries we share,

We'll keep tracing lost innocence, showing we
care,

For the missing children, for those left behind,

Their stories, their voices, forever in our mind.

Soulful Absence

In the heart of the night, where shadows creep,

A soulful absence, a secret to keep.

Invisible whispers of young lives lost,

In the dark, their innocence is the cost.

Black youth, their spirits like stars unseen,

Voyaging through night's relentless dream.

The world often turns a callous eye,

As their stories vanish into the sky.

Echoes unheard, in the depths they hide,

Their absence, a void that tears inside.

In search of answers, we trace their path,

For every lost soul, we feel their wrath.

The tears of mothers, fathers, friends,

For the departed souls, their journey never ends.

In this soulful absence, we find the strength,

To honor their memory, to go to great lengths.

The world may forget, but we will persist,

In the stories of the lost, their presence exists.

Soulful absence, we'll give you voice,

In our hearts, your memories, we'll rejoice.

In the night's embrace, their essence will rise,

As we search for the truth, beneath the skies.

For soulful absence, we'll bear the torch,

In their names, our mission we'll endorse.

In every verse, we'll keep their flame,

Their soulful absence won't bear the blame.

For they are the stars, forever they'll shine,

In our hearts and memories, for all of time.

Vanishing Youth

In a world where innocence should thrive,

Where young souls in the sun should dive,

There's a void, a silence, a painful truth,

Vanishing youth, dreams stolen in their youth.

Invisible in headlines, they disappear,

Fading whispers, nobody's tears.

Their names left unspoken, stories untold,

In the darkness, their worth unfolds.

No priority, no urgency, it seems,

For black youth lost in a world of dreams.

Their voices silenced, their futures tossed,

In the chaos, their innocence is the cost.

A puzzle of shadows, they try to decode,

The footprints left on life's heavy road.

But in the void, they search for the light,

To rekindle what was taken in the night.

A generation eclipsed, they bear the weight,

Of a world that can't see their fading state.

Yet in unity, their strength is revealed,

Their resilience, their courage, their spirit unconcealed.

Vanishing youth, your stories we share,

A silent plea in the open air.

To bring you back from the silent night,

To the world's embrace, to the shining light.

Truth in Shadows

In the dim-lit corners where the shadows stretch,

Where stories are hidden, far from public sketch,

There's a truth that lurks, concealed from the light,

A tale of injustice that we must now recite.

Invisible tears that flow from eyes unseen,

Forgotten voices of youth, just like a dream,

In the heart of the city where the streets stay cold,

Aching souls cry out for the stories untold.

Innocence vanished, stolen from their grasp,

Youthful spirits lost in this never-ending lapse,

We must seek the truth, for it is.

 buried deep,

In the hearts of families, where their sorrows seep.

With each passing day, these stories unfold,

The whispers of anguish, a truth to be told,

We can't turn away from this silent despair,

It's time to uncover the secrets hidden there.

The media may choose not to shine the light,

Law enforcement may not see it as their fight,

But in the shadows of the city where the truth remains,

The voices of the vanished cry out in silent pains.

Let us listen to their pleas, let us make a stand,

To give voice to the voiceless, lend a helping hand,

For the youth who've disappeared, it's time to reclaim,

The truth that's hidden, beneath shadows' name.

We'll cast a brighter light upon the darkness and pain,

And bring the missing youth back into life again,

In unity, we'll rise, their stories to expose,

With "Truth in Shadows," compassion surely flows.

Vanished Innocence

Eclipsed Horizons: Voices in Darkness

In the shadows of our cities, youth fades away,

Lost among the murk, swallowed by the gray,

Voices in the darkness, crying out in despair,

But will anyone listen, will someone truly care?

Eclipsed horizons, where futures should have shone,

Promises unfulfilled, dreams forever gone,

Young souls vanishing, leaving questions in their wake,

Their absence in the daylight, an unbearable heartache.

Why does the world not tremble, when they disappear?

Why does it not remember, their laughter and their tears?

These are not just numbers or faces without a name,

Each one is a universe, a unique burning flame.

Voices in the darkness, we must amplify,

Shine a light on their stories, let the truth touch the sky,

For they deserve the honor, the respect, and the grace,

Their legacies live on in the love we embrace.

Eclipsed horizons we must dispel the gloom,

In the names of the missing, we'll banish the dark's costume,

No more silenced voices, no more shadows cast,

We'll make their stories echo, in the hearts that hold them fast.

Buried Secrets: Unheard Voices Speak

In the night's quiet shroud, voices whispered, deep and bleak,

Unheard by those whose eyes averted, minds too meek.

The secrets buried beneath the surface, words left unspeakable,

As innocence faded, lost in shadows inexplicable.

A chorus of echoes from the void, they plead,

In this endless sea of darkness, their cries recede.

The young souls now vanished, seeking a guiding light,

But their stories persist, unseen, out of sight.

Behind the headlines, beneath the deafening noise,

Lies the truth obscured, hidden in the corners we forget,

Their faces may have faded, but their presence, it employs,

A relentless force, a reminder, a collective regret.

Though oblivion tried to shroud their fading tales,

Buried secrets of innocence, each heartbeat hails.

In verses, they find their voice, in songs, their cries release,

In the spoken word's embrace, these unheard voices find their peace.

As the sun sets on their struggles, they emerge from the night,

The truth prevails, even when obscured by the light.

In our hearts and minds, they'll forever resonate,

Their stories matter, and their memories we won't negate.

Gone But Not Forgotten: Missing Reflections

In the annals of time where shadows cast their veil,

The echoes of missing lives in whispers we unveil,

Gone but not forgotten, their essence still prevails,

As we ponder the reflections that their absence leaves to trail.

In the depths of this abyss, where young souls disappeared,

Innocence now cloaked in mystery, their stories oft unclear,

But we refuse to let their memory perish, to let their voices fade,

For in our hearts and verses, their presence is conveyed.

Each name a sacred utterance, every face etched in our minds,

In the gallery of missing youth, their absence leaves us blind,

But the echoes of their stories, in our verses, we shall find,

As their essence permeates the verse, their legacy is designed.

In the chorus of oblivion, we raise our voices high,

Gone but not forgotten, their stories will not die,

In the spoken word, we breathe life into the sky,

For missing reflections linger, never saying goodbye.

These young lives vanished, but their essence remains,

As we speak their names, their stories break their chains,

Gone but not forgotten, in our verses, their memory sustains,

And in our hearts, their presence forever ingrains.

SECTION 3: ECHOES OF EXPLOITATION

Vanished Innocence

Taken from Tomorrow

(Verse 1)

In the shadows of despair, where innocence resides,

A child's dreams are stolen, their bright future denied,

Silenced voices cry for help, but who's there to defend,

As the darkness lingers on, we must put it to an end.

(Chorus)

Taken from tomorrow, stolen from the light,

Invisible victims, hidden from plain sight,

Let's shine a beacon in the night, ignite the flame of grace,

For those lost in the darkness, we'll find a better place.

(Verse 2)

They were young and fragile, just like morning's dew,

Innocence and laughter, a childhood's pure debut,

But predators came lurking, with hearts devoid of care,

They took them from their dreams, leaving souls in deep despair.

(Chorus)

Taken from tomorrow, stolen from the light,

Invisible victims, hidden from plain sight,

Let's shine a beacon in the night, ignite the flame of grace,

For those lost in the darkness, we'll find a better place.

(Bridge)

We stand together, hearts entwined,

To bring back those who've been confined,

With love and hope, we'll pave the way,

To a brighter future, a brand-new day.

(Verse 3)

Let's rescue the forgotten, rewrite their tragic fate,

Healing every wounded heart, it's never too late,

United in compassion, we'll break the chains that bind,

For the ones who've suffered, leaving darkness far behind.

(Chorus)

Taken from tomorrow, stolen from the light,

Invisible victims, hidden from plain sight,

Let's shine a beacon in the night, ignite the flame of grace,

For those lost in the darkness, we'll find a better place.

(Outro)

In the echoes of exploitation, the fight has just begun,

Together we'll recover what evil thought it won,

Their stories will be told, their voices will be strong,

A world where they belong, a place where they'll belong.

Innocence for Sale

(Verse 1)

Innocence once pure and young, stolen from their grasp,

Sold like merchandise, their lives, a heavy price to clasp,

Innocence for sale, a dark and twisted trade,

Exploiting young hearts, in shadows it's displayed.

(Verse 2)

Children once full of dreams, are now trapped in a sordid game,

Deceit and treachery, a world of endless shame,

Innocence for sale, in corners, they reside,

Exploited, left in silence, as humanity divides.

(Verse 3)

Auctioned off like chattel, by those who see no wrong,

Innocence for Sale, a tragic, haunting song,

Their voices cry for freedom, their stories left untold,

Innocence for sale, a sorrow to behold.

(Verse 4)

We must shine a light on this, expose the cruel scheme,

Innocence for sale, a dark and haunting dream,

For every child who's suffered, we'll rise and take a stand,

Innocence for sale, we'll reach out our helping hand.

(Verse 5)

Their lives deserve protection, from predators who prey,

Innocence for sale, we'll fight to end this day,

In unity, we'll gather, to bring an end to this,

Innocence for sale, we'll break their dark abyss.

(Verse 6)

Innocence for sale, a grievous, bitter plight,

Exploiting young souls, in the shadows of the night,

We'll speak out for the voiceless, with courage, we'll unveil,

The innocence they've stolen, the stories they won't tell.

(Outro)

Innocence for sale, we'll stand against the tide,

For the hearts that deserve better, in their innocence, they'll find,

A future filled with hope, a world where they can heal,

Innocence is not for sale; their strength will soon be revealed.

Vanished Innocence

Invisible Chains: Unveiling the Abyss

In the shadows, youth's lost dreams entwined,

Innocence beguiled, ensnared, and maligned.

Unseen chains, their lives concealed in haze,

A web of darkness where our children gaze.

Behind the scenes, a malevolent force persists,

Expanding its dominion, clenching clenched fists.

Unveiling the abyss, the world shall now discern,

The harrowing truth, it's time for us to learn.

Through the silent suffering and hidden pain,

Invisible chains hold our youth in disdain.

Our duty clear, we'll unite,

To shatter these chains and welcome morning's light.

No more secrets, no more lurking dread,

No more tears in the quiet hours they've shed.

A global call, we rise and make a stand,

To free our children, to break the wicked hand.

In the spirit of Maya, Langston, and Dunbar's
grace,

We'll face this crisis, take our righteous place.

Together we'll stand, with courage we'll imbue,

For the voices lost, we'll unveil the truth anew.

Let the world bear witness to the change we bring,

To release our children from this vile, vile sting.

Hand in hand, we'll stride toward a brighter day,

In the footsteps of giants, we'll pave the way.

Rescued Whispers

In shadows, they once dwelled, concealed from view,

Victims of a trade that humanity barely knew.

Now rescued, but the whispers linger on,

Unseen scars, a battle fought, a war not won.

Their voices tremble, haunted by the past,

Fragments of the horrors, memories that last.

Released from chains, but still in captive minds,

The echoes of their suffering, the world seldom finds.

They were traded like commodities, innocence sold,

Invisible chains, a story left untold.

Forced into the darkness, their youth betrayed,

Innocence for sale, a debt that can't be repaid.

The rescue came, a glimmer of hope's embrace,

Yet, the scars remain, etched on their face.

Invisible chains, tightly bound within,

The trauma lingers, beneath the fragile skin.

Their voices, like whispers, too fragile to reveal,

The torment they've endured, their hearts concealed.

But we must listen, be a guiding hand,

Rescue their whispers from the shadows' cruel command.

With empathy and love, we'll mend their shattered souls,

Their voices will grow stronger as healing takes its toll.

Rescued whispers rising, breaking free from fear,

In unity and strength, their truth will reappear.

We stand beside them, hearts open wide,

To help them find the strength to heal inside.

Rescued from the darkness, they'll find their way,

Whispers growing stronger, their strength displayed.

Vanished Innocence

SECTION 4: THE SILENT EPIDEMIC

The Hidden Trade

In shadows deep, a chilling trade unfolds,

A macabre market where human suffering is sold.

Black lives, unspoken tales, the price we pay,

As the sinister underworld claims its prey.

Organs stolen in the darkest of nights,

Taken from those who vanished from our sight,

Their stories hushed, concealed in a void,

While this heinous industry profits, unalloyed.

Innocence, stolen, dignity defiled,

Innocent hearts lured, entrapped, reviled.

The hidden trade preys upon the vulnerable,

A clandestine empire, cold and terrible.

Families left to mourn, in silence they weep,

As missing loved ones vanish into the deep.

Their pain, a testament to the silent war,

The hidden trade, an evil like never before.

A call for action, a plea to unveil,

The secrets hidden behind this twisted tale.

For every life lost in this sinister scheme,

We'll shed light on the hidden trade's dark regime.

Uncover the truth, expose the vile trade,

In the memory of those lost, our voices will cascade.

A silent epidemic that must be revealed,

To protect the innocent and allow wounds to heal.

.

Bodies for Profit

In the underbelly of society, a dreadful scheme does dwell,

Where human lives are commodified, their fate in the hands of those who sell.

They prey on innocence, with greed their only creed,

Trading bodies like merchandise, is a sinister human need.

The auction block is hidden, concealed from the public's eye,

Where black lives are bought and sold, in silence they will die.

Their organs harvested for gain, a grotesque form of trade,

As human lives are stolen, in darkness they cascade.

Innocent souls unknowingly caught in this sinister plot,

Lured by false promises, their hopes soon forgot.

Trapped in a nightmare of deception and despair,

Their cries go unheard, their anguish too much to bear.

Families were left to wonder, where did their loved ones go?

The answer lies in this secret market, where dark shadows grow.

We must confront this epidemic, expose the wicked truth,

For every stolen life, we must stand and raise our voices.

Bodies for profit, a horrifying reality we face,

But together we'll fight this darkness and bring justice to this place.

In the memory of those taken, we'll uncover the vile scheme,

And stop the trade that preys on lives from being an ongoing theme.

Pricing Humanity

In a world where value is weighed by the dollar's cruel hand,

Humanity's up for sale, a sinister, grim command.

Beneath the shadows' grasp, a chilling bazaar unfurls,

Where lives are auctioned off, in this heartless underworld.

They trade in souls like chattel, a grotesque, shadowy trade,

Where vulnerable hearts are the currency paid.

Price tags on existence, on stolen dreams, they write,

For every heart they've harvested, another sleepless night.

They profit from the agony, they care not for the cost,

Innocence and virtue, as commodities, are tossed.

Their greed knows no bounds, as lives are bought and sold,

In this heartless marketplace, where morality's grown cold.

Behind the scenes, the anguish, a pain we cannot erase,

As they price humanity with a callous, heartless embrace.

But we'll raise our voices, expose this gruesome trade,

To protect our brothers and sisters, the debt must be repaid.

We'll unveil the darkness, the silent epidemic's might,

As we stand for every soul, whose innocence they slight.

With unity, compassion, and love, we will strive,

To reclaim our stolen humanity and make all hearts come alive.

With hope in our hearts, we'll unveil the truth, you'll see,

No life should bear a price; we must all forever be free.

Reflections in Verse

Stolen Lives, Stolen Organs

In the hidden chambers of despair, a heinous trade thrives,

A nefarious exchange where stolen hopes and dreams derive.

Once vibrant lives, now trapped in this twisted web,

Their destinies intertwined in darkness, where virtue's lifeblood ebbs.

From the depths of innocence, stolen away by vile intent,

They navigate the abyss, their purity now misspent.

A world that preys on fragility, in the secrecy it thrives,

As innocence is up for sale, and morality takes a dive.

Innocence for sale, a chilling narrative unfolds,

Where hearts and spirits are bartered, and no compassion holds.

With no regard for humanity, it reaps a wicked toll,

Leaving behind a trail of despair, a life forever stole.

In the hidden corners of despair, their voices softly cry,

Yet unheard, they linger on, in the shadows they rely.

Families left in anguish, their hearts forever scarred,

Bearing the weight of sorrow, their lives forever marred.

Stolen lives, stolen organs, a grim and haunting tale,

A market of malevolence where humanity is frail.

In the depths of obscurity, their stories must be voiced,

To shine a light on this darkness, to make an empowered choice.

No more stolen lives, no more organs for sale,

Together, we'll rise against this malevolent travail.

In the name of justice, the truths we must unveil,

For those who've been victimized, their stories shall prevail.

In unity and strength, as a formidable brigade,

We'll dismantle this horror, as its remorse will fade.

We'll end the reign of terror, the stolen lives shall ascend,

Their voices will be heard, and their pain will mend.

In the hidden trade of innocence, we'll expose the blight,

Bringing hope to those who've suffered, ensuring their respite.

No more stolen lives, no more stolen organs, we vow,

To safeguard the vulnerable, to bring justice here and now.

In the face of darkness, we'll ignite the truth's bright flame,

With compassion as our armor, we'll conquer every aim.

Searching for Answers

In the heart of the darkness, where questions quietly wail,

Families and communities yearn for truths to unveil.

Their voices echo through the night, a plea that's hard to bear,

Searching for answers, in a world that's unaware.

With each name that disappears, their anguish does increase,

They seek to comprehend the mysteries, to find their inner peace.

The media turns a blind eye, and law enforcement is detached,

Leaving families in the shadows, their voices being unmatched.

Invisible are the stories of these lives that slip away,

As communities stand vigilant, their hopes and dreams in disarray.

They're searching for answers, their courage undeterred,

To shed light on the truth, in a world that's oft unheard.

The void is filled with questions, as they journey through the night,

Seeking solace in the answers, to make the wrongs all right.

But the questions lead to silence, where shadows tightly cling,

And the truth remains elusive, in a symphony of suffering.

Yet, united they persist, a relentless, boundless force,

In their quest for understanding, on a determined, unwavering course.

For the lives that went missing, in the shadow's deep abyss,

They keep searching for answers, with hope they won't dismiss.

Their voices rise in unity, like a chorus in the dark,

Families and communities leave their indelible mark.

In the face of this silence, they'll rise and take a stand,

Searching for answers, to reclaim what's buried in the sand.

In the heart of the darkness, where questions softly cry,

They'll press on in their mission, with resilience to defy.

For in the unity of voices, they'll find their way through the night,

Searching for answers, to bring the truth to light.

Reflections in Verse

Black Market Horrors: The Trail of Vanishing Lives

Beneath the veil of night, where secrets slowly creep,

Lies a twisted market, where lives are bought and sold, so deep.

Hidden from the world, a dark and wretched trade,

Where black lives disappear, on a path that's so betrayed.

The trail of vanishing lives, marked by sorrow and despair,

A market thriving on the innocent, a wicked, callous snare.

Innocence is stolen, and dreams are cast aside,

As this black-market feeds upon, with hearts and souls denied.

From the street corners to hidden dens, the hunt for profit grows,

With ruthless hands and cold intentions, the sinister story flows.

Innocence is the currency, in this market of despair,

Leaving hearts forever scarred, with a heavy cross to bear.

Families left in anguish, with unanswered questions near,

As the trail of vanishing lives erases futures once so clear.

The horrors of the black market, a sinister, chilling tale,

Of stolen youth and silenced voices, where innocence turns pale.

The market thrives in shadows, where black lives disappear,

As the world remains oblivious, to the cries they cannot hear.

But we stand in unity, to expose this dark disguise,

To end the black-market horrors, where innocence often dies.

With courage and determination, we'll break these heavy chains,

Bring light into the darkness, where despair forever reigns.

For the trail of vanishing lives, we'll strive to set things right,

To bring justice to the innocent and end their endless night.

Beneath the surface of the earth, where secrets slowly creep,

Lies the trail of vanishing lives, where promises are incomplete.

In the face of black-market horrors, we'll join our voices high,

To save the stolen innocence and reveal the twisted lie.

Reflections in Verse

SECTION 5: HOLDING THE MIRROR TO BIAS'

Reflections in Verse

Hidden Realities: Seeking Fairness

In a world where bias shadows the view,

We unveil the truth, and seek what's due,

When our loved ones vanish, we face despair,

Inequalities in search, an unjust affair.

Yearning for fairness, we stand our ground,

Our voices heard, a clarion sound,

The mirror reflects the disparities we see,

In the face of bias, we strive to break free.

With eyes wide open, we challenge the scheme,

Demanding justice, we won't let it deem,

Our devotion is unwavering, a passionate flame,

In a world where equity holds no shame.

Hidden realities, we confront the strife,

To mend the divide and better life,

For our missing beloved, our hearts burn,

As we seek fairness, we fervently yearn.

The bias unmasked, we'll persevere,

United and resolute, we hold it dear,

In pursuit of justice, the chains shall sever,

Revealing the love in our hearts forever.

Hidden truths laid bare, we'll fight the plight,

Seeking fairness, we'll unite and ignite,

A world where justice knows no restraint,

In unity's embrace, a brighter world we'll paint.

Untold Stories: A Quest for Equity

In shadows cast by bias's pall,

Untold stories rise, a haunting call,

Inequity's grip on hearts and minds,

Where missing children leave no signs.

We quest for equity, a balance fair,

In searching for our loved ones, we dare,

To rise above the prejudiced divide,

For equal treatment, we'll not hide.

Each missing child, a precious soul,

Their stories matter, they make us whole,

The demand for justice in each plea,

For all our children, set them free.

In unity, we seek to find,

A world where bias is left behind,

Untold stories no longer confined,

In our quest for equity, we bind.

The Missing Headlines

In the stark luminescence of the public's gaze,

A narrative concealed, hidden from the craze,

Within the chronicles of printed text,

Some tales vanish, leaving us perplexed.

While the media's lens captures the elite,

Others remain in the margins, incomplete,

The missing, black youth, their voices unheard,

Their stories concealed, like a forgotten word.

"The Missing Headline," an untold report,

Invisible narratives unjustly kept short,

We advocate for an impartial decree,

To unveil young black lives cloaked in mystery.

In obscurity, they linger, neglected, unseen,

Black lives, society's victims it deems,

We'll amplify their voices from the shade,

Till no vanished child is left to fade.

Unseen Pleas: The Media's Silent Lens

Beneath the cover of media's craft,

Lies an obscure tale, seemingly daft,

Unheard echoes of parents' aching cries,

Their missing children in silent demise.

The lens fixates on tales deemed bright,

But veils the plight, shunning the night,

Darker hues, a glance cast away,

Black lives were lost in the sun's harsh rays.

Silenced pleas from those in need,

Their children's fate, they cannot heed,

Unspoken whispers, a silent lament,

Untold stories that demand ascent.

In this verse, a mature stance I take,

To shed light on lives deemed opaque,

Each word, a call for a balanced view,

To highlight lives that need voices, too.

Media's Selective Echo

In the media's chamber, a narrative spin,

Selective echoes where the bias begins,

Reverberating tales of fairer complexion,

While the cries of black lives face sheer rejection.

A cacophony of voices, clamoring for a sound,

But the media's favor plays in the background,

Echoing the stories of one hue, it's clear,

The same courtesy for others is nowhere near.

In the quest for truth and equal regard,

Black lives vanish in shadows, their stories barred,

The media's selective echo we must confront,

For every missing life deserves a resonating front.

A clarion call to break these chains,

And in every newsroom, new perspectives gain,

For every life is precious, every story must be
heard,

Media's selective echo, let it no longer be the word.

The media's role is crucial, this is true,

But when it comes to black lives, there's much more to do,

Stories unheard, voices suppressed, it's time to break the mold,

For every missing child, let their stories be told.

This world is diverse, its people unique,

Let's amplify each voice, let their stories speak,

In unity and fairness, let the media stand,

Media's selective echo, we must change, and expand.

Law Enforcement's Apathy

In the heart of the city, where shadows roam free,

A mother stands frantic, where no one can see,

She pleads with the heavens, to bring back her child,

But to law enforcement, her tears are beguiled.

Her trembling voice speaks, with a raw, wrenching cry,

Yet officers brush her off, in the blink of an eye,

Her child's gone missing, like a whisper, a ghost,

But to them, she's just one, a nameless, lost host.

They nod and they promise, their words slick as oil,

But behind closed doors, they barely give toil,

For her child has dark skin, that's the only crime,

That keeps their hearts guarded, oblivious to time.

They ask few questions, her story brushed aside,

Apathy and neglect, where her hopes slowly died,

With dismissive glances and negligent ears,

Her child's life slipping through, dissolving in fears.

Her pleas turned to whispers, unheard in the night,

With hope dwindling away, like the last flicker of light,

Invisible cries for help, fell on deaf ears,

As law enforcement turned a blind eye to her tears.

Her child's worth, unseen in their prejudiced glance,

Just another statistic, lost in the dance,

Of a system that fails to protect and to serve,

Leaving parents in anguish, their hearts in a curve.

The tragedy lies in the deep bias concealed,

In the hearts of some officers, their duty unsealed,

To protect all, serve all, without judgment or spite,

To acknowledge each life and their sacred right.

The system needs mending, a change in its core,

To ensure that all parents are treated as more,

Then mere faces in shadows, with children unseen,

But as voices of hope, in this world so serene.

Law enforcement's apathy, a cry to be heard,

To shatter the silence, let their hearts be stirred,

To see the worth in each life, regardless of hue,

And bring back the lost, for justice is due.

Reflections in Verse

Dismissed Tears: A Cry for Recognition

In the heart of despair, where the shadows
convene,

Lives a mother, her face masked by anguish,
unseen,

Her child, a young soul, lost in the night,

Yet the world turns a blind eye, no help in her
sight.

She pleads and she prays to the heavens above,

But her cries are ignored, like a mourning dove,

Her tears fall like rain, in the still of the night,

An endless lament, in the absence of light.

To the doorstep of justice, she drags her despair,

But they dismiss her tears as if they're not aware,

Of the agony she carries, her pain left unheard,

In the world's apathy, her heart is interred.

They ask her questions, but they're cursory, brief,

As if her child's worth is a fading motif,

Their indifference cuts deep, like a knife through her soul,

While her child's whereabouts, the darkness still stole.

She's a voice in the shadows, a face without name,

In a world that looks past her, in their hunt for fame,

They find other stories, their headlines so bright,

But her child's life story, fading out of sight.

Her cries go unanswered, a silence profound,

As law enforcement's echoes create a deep mound,

Of injustice and prejudice, a divide that's so wide,

Where black lives are diminished, their worth set aside.

But she's more than a tear, more than a plea,

She's a mother in mourning, who's yearning to see,

Her child once again, under the sun's warm embrace,

With the world as her witness, she won't be erased.

For the tears she has shed, the pain she has borne,

Deserve to be seen, in the light of the morn,

Her cries for recognition, a battle to fight,

As her child's life story deserves to ignite.

Reflections in Verse

Searching Alone: Disregarded Cries

In the depths of the night, a mother weeps alone,

Her child's gone missing, into the unknown,

She reaches out for help, to those who should care,

But her tears fall unnoticed, in a world unfair.

Her voice cries out for answers, for a glimmer of hope,

But the world turns a deaf ear, it's a slippery slope,

Her heart's heavy with sorrow, a burden so deep,

As she searches alone, in the night's restless sleep.

Law enforcement's indifference, a heavy chain to bear,

For the truth they don't seek, her cries they don't hear,

She's left in the shadows, a mother in despair,

As her tears go unheeded, in the cold, callous air.

She's not alone in her anguish, this pain she
endures,

For many like her, the pain's unjust, it's not theirs,

With disregarded tears, they search for a trace,

Of their loved ones gone missing, in this heartless
chase.

In a world that's divided, her voice must be strong,

To bridge the deep chasm, where her child
belongs,

She demands recognition, for the pain that she
bears,

For the tears that she sheds, for the love that she
swears.

Torn Apart: The Battle for Belief

In the haunted spaces where belief's battle
ensues,

A mother holds on to faith, despite the world's
dark hues,

Her child is torn away, lost in life's bitter fray,

Her belief in truth, unwavering, amid the disarray.

The world denies her pleas, the whispers of her
fears,

In the void of unseen trust, in the well of silent
tears,

She's searching for conviction, for the power of
belief,

In the face of shattered hope, in the chasm of grief.

Her cries echo in silence, the disbelief profound,

As the world looks away, in disbelief unbound,

But her heart holds a flame, a beacon through the
storm,

The belief in her child becomes her only norm.

Her battle for belief is a struggle to reveal,

The truth, the cries, the love that's so very real,

To part the clouds of doubt, to let the light shine through,

To honor her lost child, her love strong and true.

The Struggle Against Indifference

In the search for lost youth, a glaring divide is unveiled,

Where a child's vanished presence seems unfairly assailed.

Equality beckons from the heart of the unknown,

Yearning for fairness for all, every child, every home.

When a black child's absence fills the air,

There's a stark contrast, a contrasting care.

In the media's echo, in the law's call,

The response isn't equal, it's a startling fall.

In the headlines, a disproportionate glance,

A white face may find priority and chance,

While countless black children's faces fade away,

Their names, their stories, lost in the fray.

But the heart doesn't distinguish in color or hue,

When it's torn, it aches just the same, it's true.

In every home, where a child is adored,

The desperation for answers is the common chord.

The collective yearning for equality's reign,

Where race and shade won't dictate the pain.

For every lost child, let the rallying cry sound,

Unifying the search till every child is found.

Together, our voices, a united plea,

A shout for fairness, equality to decree.

For the struggle against indifference to mend,

All missing children, a nation to defend.

In the embrace of equal empathy's embrace,

May every missing child find their rightful place.

In society's eyes, regardless of skin,

Equal hope, effort, and search should begin.

Us vs Them: When Race Defines Response

In the realm of the missing, a stark divide appears,

When race becomes a factor, the truth is crystal clear.

Though every heartache shares the same despair,

A contrast in response shows an unequal care.

For when a child with darker skin is reported gone,

The urgency and attention seem weaker, withdrawn.

As if a racial filter clouds society's sight,

A bias lurking in the shadows, shrouded in the night.

But a child's worth transcends the hue of their skin,

It's the heartache that unites, from deep within.

In every parent's eyes, the same tears fall,

A common anguish shared by one and all.

The media's echo, a selective response,

Favoring headlines where whiteness takes its chance.

While countless black lives vanish into the abyss,

Their stories eclipsed, an unnoticed miss.

But this isn't a battle we should fight alone,

United we stand, to change what's been overthrown.

In the quest to find our missing youth,

It's unity and fairness that reveal the truth.

A collective cry for equality to resound,

To bridge the gap, on level ground.

In a world where the response is colorblind,

Every missing child is worth the find.

Let's rewrite the narrative, reclaim the lost,

Where race won't define what it may cost.

In the quest for all missing children to defend,

May our unity shatter the barriers, and mend.

Vanished Innocence

Reflections in Verse

Color-Coded Neglect

In the shadows of despair, a story oft untold,

A tapestry of anguish, where darkness takes its hold.

Where hearts of ebony are left to bear the weight,

Of color-coded neglect, an unequal twist of fate.

Law enforcement's silence in the face of our distress,

A pattern of indifference, an issue we must address.

With tears that stain the pavement and voices often unheard,

The struggle for a brighter path, our hope and truth conferred.

As media selectively decides whose story to embrace,

Black lives are overshadowed, erased without a trace.

While headlines blaze for others, their narratives well-fed,

We mourn the silence cast upon our sons and daughters, dead.

But together we can rise, against this bias, stand and fight,

To shed light on this injustice, to make our wrongs turn right.

In unity, we'll overcome the darkness that we've known,

Color-coded neglect, no more—our voices louder, grown.

For every missing life, of any shade, we must defend,

The hue of skin won't dictate the worth of children, in the end.

Let's challenge bias with unity, demand the world respect,

That justice isn't color-coded; our message, we'll project.

In the face of neglect, we'll rise and redefine,

A future where compassion and equality will shine.

Our stories won't be silenced, our voices, we'll protect,

A world where love transcends, and color-coded neglect.

Reflections in Verse

EmpowerEqual:

(Shedding light on the disparities in media coverage and law enforcement responses, while also advocating for a more equitable and compassionate approach to missing persons cases. I chose to encapsulate the essence of this section and ensure it serves as an awareness and a call to action).

In recent years, the cases of missing individuals have captured the attention of the public and sparked nationwide concern and calls for their safe return. While the public outcry for missing persons is an encouraging sign of compassion and solidarity, there is a stark contrast in the level of attention and support these cases receive based on the race of the individuals involved.

The stark example of this disparity lies in the cases of Gabby Petito and Jelani Day. Gabby Petito's case garnered significant media coverage and widespread public support, with countless people following the updates on social media and news outlets. On the other hand, Jelani Day, an African American graduate student who went missing around the same time as Gabby, received considerably less attention.

This discrepancy is a manifestation of what has been termed the "missing White woman syndrome." It reflects the disproportionate media coverage and public sympathy afforded to cases involving missing White women, while cases involving people of color, particularly Black and Indigenous individuals, often go overlooked. This discrepancy is not merely a matter of statistics but has life-altering consequences.

In the United States in 2022, approximately 546,568 individuals were reported as missing. Out of this staggering number, nearly 39% were Black people. However, the response to these cases is far from equitable. Law enforcement frequently classifies missing Black children as runaways, a designation that precludes issuing amber alerts, depriving these cases of immediate public awareness.

This differential treatment is further exacerbated when these children are presumed to have voluntarily left. Authorities often allocate fewer resources to find them, operating under the assumption that they will likely run away again once located. This unjust bias perpetuates an alarming cycle, leaving Black families without the same level of support and attention afforded to their White counterparts.

The problem extends to cases involving missing adults as well. Many missing Black adults are unfairly labeled as being involved in criminal activities. These cases are underreported and overlooked, hampering the efforts of family members trying to locate their loved ones. This is not an isolated issue, as multiple cases, like the 2009 disappearance of 11 women in Cleveland, reflect the same pattern of dismissive treatment by law enforcement.

The persistent lack of media attention and insufficient resources allocated to communities of color places missing individuals at greater risk. Families left to navigate the complexities of searching for their missing loved ones often find themselves on an arduous journey with minimal institutional support.

This problem extends beyond the borders of the United States. The crisis of Missing and Murdered Indigenous Women is a deeply alarming issue, particularly in the United States and Canada. The homicide rate for Indigenous women is approximately six times higher than that for White women. Despite this, their cases receive 27 times less newsprint coverage, and the coverage tends to be clinical and impersonal. The lack of media attention, coupled with inadequate resources and support, significantly reduces the chances of resolving these cases.

The disparities in media coverage, public support, and law enforcement response are deeply concerning. They reflect a systemic problem that endangers the lives of individuals of color, particularly Black and Indigenous communities. It's essential to address this issue by advocating for equitable treatment of all missing persons, regardless of their racial or ethnic background.

In conclusion, every missing person deserves to have their case taken seriously and receive the public's attention and concern. While it's crucial to ensure that missing White women receive the support they need, the same level of compassion and resources should be extended to the thousands of other missing people whose stories don't receive the same level of attention. The media plays a vital role in raising awareness about missing persons, but it can only achieve its purpose when every story is treated with equal responsibility and empathy. A more equitable approach to reporting and responding to missing persons' cases is not only a moral imperative but a necessary step toward creating a just and compassionate society.

Here is One last poem offering these facts as well:

EmpowerEqual Poem

In a world where disparities persist,

Where the cries for help and justice exist,

The case of Gabby Petito, so widely known,

Yet for many like Jelani Day, the concern is hardly shown.

Invisible crises unfold in plain sight,

As people of color go missing, day and night.

The missing White woman syndrome, it's called,

While Black lives vanish, their stories often stalled.

Though thousands disappear every year,

Black folks comprise a significant share, we fear.

But in most cases, they're quickly labeled "runaways,"

Which means no amber alerts, no national gaze.

Black families left to search on their own,

Their cries for help seemingly overthrown.

A lack of media attention, the resources denied,

Makes finding these missing children a treacherous ride.

Black children are often assumed to run away,

Their cases don't receive the same priority, we say.

Police departments less likely to engage,

In searching for kids, they believe will escape.

The disappearance of presumed criminals as well,

Falls into a dark and unjust spell.

Labeled as such, their stories remain untold,

Their cases left in shadows, growing cold.

The public becomes desensitized,

When crime is the image that's always realized.

Their empathy wanes, the help doesn't come,

Leaving families in despair, feeling so numb.

But media should paint a broader view,

Including all stories, making empathy accrue.

Emergency departments should be better trained,

To identify missing persons, and not be constrained.

The Missing and Murdered Indigenous Women's plight,

Is another tragedy that demands the light.

Their cases, rarely personal, rarely seen,

While their families are caught in a nightmare's dream.

Though poor coverage is part of the tale,

The disparities grow due to a system's fail.

Indigenous women don't get the same support,

Families left wondering, a painful retort.

Their cases remain unsolved, a chilling truth,

When lives are at stake, the urgency of our youth.

More coverage, attention, and care we must give,

To ensure their safety and let these families live.

Every missing person, regardless of their race,

Deserves attention, a spotlight on their case.

The media can be a powerful tool for all to see,

But it must serve every story, each plea.

So, let's advocate for change, and equality we must share,

The disparities in missing persons, the burden we bear.

All missing lives deserve care and concern,

Their safety and well-being are lessons we need to learn.

THANK YOU

As I conclude this book, "Reflections in Verse, Volume 7: Vanished Innocence," I want to express my heartfelt gratitude to those who have been part of this journey. The creation of this volume has been a labor of love and an opportunity to give voice to the voiceless.

Thank you to all the families who have endured the heart-wrenching experience of having a loved one go missing, especially those from the Black community who face unique challenges in their search for answers.

To the activists and advocates who tirelessly work to bring awareness to these issues, your dedication is inspiring.

I want to acknowledge the countless missing individuals whose stories remain untold. You are not forgotten, and your stories continue to shape the narrative for future generations.

My appreciation goes out to all the readers who have chosen to engage with this work, to reflect upon the issues presented, and to consider the importance of empathy and equal treatment for all.

Lastly, a special thank you to the Black and Missing Foundation and all organizations dedicated to supporting the families of missing individuals.

May this book serve as a call to action, a catalyst for change, and a testament to the resilience of those who seek truth and justice. Together, we can strive for a world where every missing person receives the attention and care they deserve.

With deepest gratitude,

Khalilah H. Purnell

ABOUT THE AUTHOR

Khalilah H. Purnell is a distinguished author, poet, and relentless advocate with a profound dedication to amplifying the voices of those who are often left in silence. Khalilah's roots extend across different regions and communities, providing her with a diverse and well-rounded perspective. Her journey began with a fascination for the potency of words, a fascination that has evolved into a lifelong mission.

Khalilah's writing traverses various themes but always circles back to her central focus: justice, equality, and social reform. Her body of work encompasses a broad spectrum of literary creations, each designed to shed light on critical issues, cultivate empathy, and inspire action. Her narratives are not merely words on a page but a catalyst for change.

With every piece she pens, Khalilah H. Purnell channels her deep-seated belief in the power of storytelling to drive societal transformation. Beyond her literary prowess, she is recognized for her unwavering commitment to advocating for marginalized communities, particularly within the Black diaspora.

Khalilah's work represents a tireless crusade, demanding the unheard voices be acknowledged and heeded. "Reflections in Verse, Volume 7: Vanished Innocence" stands as a powerful testament to Khalilah's lifelong dedication to using her writing to catalyze change and foster unity.

Contact/Booking Information

For inquiries, interviews, speaking engagements, appearances, or literary opportunities, please get in touch with Author the team for Khalilah H. Purnell at:

Email: khalilahhpurnell@gmail.com

Website: www.khalilahhpurnell.com

Social Media:

Facebook: Khalilah H. Purnell Author

LinkedIn: https://www.linkedin.com/in/khalilahpurnell/

Instagram: @khalilahhpurnell

Khalilah H. Purnell is open to speaking engagements, collaborations, and literary projects aimed at giving voice to the silenced and fostering change. For booking inquiries or to discuss potential collaborations, please use the provided contact information.

Reflections in Verse

Milton Keynes UK
Ingram Content Group UK Ltd.
UKHW010243221123
432980UK00003B/275

9 798868 990526